THE ART OF **INDIA**

NIGEL CAWTHORNE

BARNES
& NOBLE

NEW YORK

Copyright © Octopus Publishing Group Ltd 1997, 2006

First published in 1997 by Hamlyn,
a division of Octopus Publishing Group Ltd

This 2006 edition published by Barnes & Noble, Inc. by
arrangement with Bounty Books, a division of Octopus
Publishing Group Ltd.

Publishing Director: Laura Bamford
Executive Editor: Mike Evans
Editor: Humaira Husain
Art Director: Keith Martin
Senior Designer: Geoff Borin
Design: Birgit Eggers
Production Controller: Mark Walker
Picture Research: Charlotte Deane

ISBN-13: 978-0-7607-8876-9
ISBN-10: 0-7607-8876-6

A CIP catalogue record for this book is available
from the British Library

Printed and bound in China

1 3 5 7 9 10 8 6 4 2

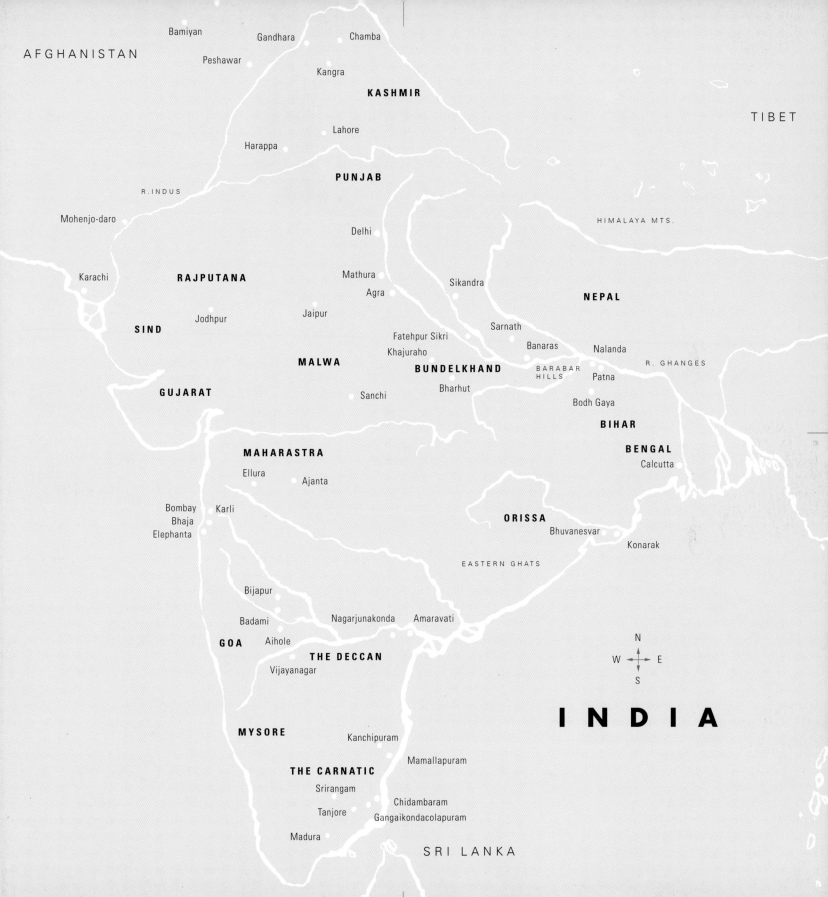

The Indian subcontinent is the home of one of the world's oldest civilizations. Urban culture first flowered there around 2500 BC. From that early beginning Indian art has exhibited an extraordinary consistency, despite successive invasions and the influence of a multiplicity of religions: **Islam, Hinduism, Buddhism** and **Jainism** have all played their part. The essential characteristics of Indian art are also much the same, whether expressed in paint, clay, wood, metal, stone or brick. And this singular artistic vision has been a potent export. Its influence can be seen in the art and architecture of Sri Lanka, Burma (Myanmar), Thailand, Indonesia, Cambodia, Laos and Vietnam.

The source of this coherent vision is the Indian village, which has changed little down the centuries. To this day, Hindu villagers worship mother goddesses made from straw and cow dung just as they did thousands of years ago. Terracotta figurines, handmade pottery, dyed fabrics and children's kites crafted in Indian villages still carry ancient emblems and symbols that are the inspiration behind the rich icons of the Hindu pantheon and reach far back into India's prehistory. However, the importance of Indian art was long overlooked in the West. Early European visitors were often offended by its erotic content. To them, its lack of perspective and disregard of realism made it seem primitive. But Indian artists were not attempting to portray the world they saw around them.

They regarded the world as an illusion and through their art were endeavouring to reveal the truth behind it.

Indian art is full of symbolism drawn from one of the richest, most sophisticated cultures in the world. The meanings that animate that culture are now being understood in the West and Indian art can at last be seen and appreciated in its full glory.

The imposing profile of the Jami Masjid, the largest mosque in India, and one of the great buildings of Delhi created in the 17th century by Shah Jahan

1 — THE ART OF THE INDUS VALLEY

The story of Indian art begins with the civilization that developed in the Indus Valley in the 3rd millennium BC. Like the early civilizations in Egypt and Sumeria, it grew up along a river that flooded seasonally. This was good for agriculture, but bad for architecture.

The ruins of the city of Mohenjo-daro on the Indus delta, cradle of early Indian civilization and art

The soapstone bust of a man, thought to be a king priest, unearthed at Mohenjo-daro

The culture was named after Harappa in Punjab, which was the first of its ancient cities to be discovered. Harappan culture was not, however, confined to this particular place. The city of **Mohenjo-daro**, near to the delta of the Indus, dates from the same era. At its height, the Indus Valley civilization extended along the coast of Baluchistan and Gujarat and inland across Rajasthan and down the fertile land between the Ganges and Jumna rivers.

Little is known of the inhabitants of these cities. Hindu texts talk of the mighty citadels built by broad-nosed, dark skinned people who worshipped the phallus. The pottery they left behind them is similar to that from ancient Persia, suggesting they came from the west. According to the Vedic scriptures, they were eventually overwhelmed by the Aryan armies under the banner of the 'Hurler of the Thunderbolt', the lord of heaven, Indra. They became slaves and may possibly be the ancestors of the Dravidian peoples of south India and Sri Lanka. The city of Harappa was discovered in 1856 during the construction of a railway in Punjab. Unfortunately, it had been largely destroyed. Mohenjo-daro was found in 1922 and was still mainly intact. Each city, which had around 35,000 inhabitants, was laid out on a grid pattern and had an advanced drainage system. The most striking feature of these cities – and other Harappan sites such as Kalibangan in Rajasthan – was the raised citadel, standing some 40 to 50 ft (12 to 15 m) above the rest of the city. Although the houses had their own private bathrooms, each city had a huge public bath, sealed with bitumen and surrounded by a courtyard. These may have been water tanks to catch the monsoon rains, but were more likely used for ritual bathing.

The most widespread of their artefacts are small **soapstone seals**. These are square tablets 1.5 to 3 in (38 to 76 mm) high used as a stamp of ownership on goods. Each seal had an emblem cut into it in reverse relief. The emblem is usually an animal. Tigers, elephants, rhinoceroses, crocodiles, hares, antelope and water buffalo all appear, but the most popular was the Brahmani bull. Sometimes there are grotesque, multi-headed or composite animals, suggesting that the seals have some religious significance. Human figures occasionally appear, but they are crude and primitive compared with the animals. Other symbols including swastikas, crosses, patterns of dots, circles and the leaves of the sacred bodhi tree were also used. Above the emblem some words appear in a script that is now indecipherable. The carved stone was covered in alkali and fired to a shiny white finish. A pierced stud on the back allowed a cord to be attached, so possibly these seals were worn as jewellery. Thousands of them have been found, some as far away as Bahrain and Mesopotamia, indicating that the people of the Indus Valley were involved in international trade. The most famous seal was discovered at Mohenjo-daro. It shows the god **Shiva** sitting in a yoga position on a throne, with his phallus prominently displayed. A great number of stone phalluses were found in the city. These were fertility symbols, but were also traditionally identified with Shiva.

The steatite, or soapstone, seal, showing the god Shiva, discovered at Mohenjo-daro

A typical seal featuring an elephant, decorated with a bodhi leaf and fishes

A red sandstone male torso and grey sandstone male dancer, both found at Harappa, and dating from between 2300 and 1750 BC

Shiva's throne is supported by lions – an image used both in Buddhist and Jain art. There are also two deer under the throne which, again, is a symbol associated with Buddhism. A bust of a man carved in soapstone was also found at Mohenjo-daro. He has a broad nose and thick lips – identifying him as one of the defeated people described in Hindu texts. He is wearing a toga with a three-leafed design, which was also common in Crete, Egypt and Mesopotamia. His hair is tied back in a bun. His beard is well groomed and his upper lip is shaved. Another small statue was found at Harappa. This figure is made out of red limestone and it depicts a **male torso**. It is highly realistic and, since much Indian art is usually highly stylized it has been suggested that it was infact an import from the Mediterranean.

However, in place of the flat stomachs of Greek statues, this sculpture has a rounded belly, an Indian symbol of well-being.

A similar realistic image of the twisted torso of a male dancer, made in grey limestone, was also found at Harappa. The legs are broken and the head and arms, which once fitted into drilled sockets at the neck and shoulders, are missing. Also missing is the phallus.

Statuettes were also made from bronze or copper. The most famous from this period is the small copper figure of a **dancing girl** found at Mohenjo-daro. It was cast using the lost-wax process, in which the sculpture is first made in wax. Then a mould is made by coating the wax with clay. When the clay is heated, the wax melts and runs out as the molten metal takes its place. The girl is naked except for some jewellery – a necklace and an armful of bangles. Her pose and her expression are both delightfully relaxed. She, too, has a flattened nose and thick lips, helping to identify her from the early Hindu texts.

The copper statuette of a dancing girl originating from Mohenjo-daro, now in the National Museum of India, New Delhi

A terracotta flying bird, tortoise and squirrel, from Chanhudaro, just south of Mohenjo-daro on the delta of the Indus river

Another animal seal, this one depicting a rhinoceros and symbols above which include a butterfly

Clay was the most widely used material within the Indus Valley civilization. The cities were built paved in kiln-fired brick, a tradition that continues in Sind and Punjab to this day. The potter's wheel, first used by Sumerians in the 24th century BC, was used to make beakers, storage jars, perforated strainers, dishes that stood on a pedestal and goblets with a pointed base that could be stuck in the ground. Sometimes these have a creamy finish, but more usually are coated in red slip with a black design painted over it. The designs are often complex abstract patterns of lines, checks and circles. Occasionally, bodhi leaves, fish, bulls, peacocks and other animals appear. Human figures, again, are crudely rendered. There are also many **modelled pieces**. Some are toys, others votive offerings or even idols to be worshipped. Among them are a large number of **'mother goddesses'** with large breasts and wide hips. These are covered in jewellery and have large head-dresses, which sometimes doubled as the cavity for a lamp.

It is clear from the archaeological record that, even before the Aryans arrived, the civilization of the Indus Valley had been in a long decline. The land was slowly rising and the flow of the Indus and its flooding became erratic. The Harappan trading ports along the coast are now far inland. Mohenjo-daro found itself in the middle of a brackish lake.

Then, around 1700 BC, the **Aryans** came with bronze weapons and chariots. They swept down the Indus Valley meeting little resistance. In Mohenjo-daro a family of nine ivory carvers, five of them children, were found slaughtered next to two tusks. Survivors of the Aryan onslaught fled into the hills or jungles or were driven south. Some may have regressed to the stone age. The earliest cave paintings in India

date from around 5500 BC, however in the south, the Neolithic culture continued until the Christian era.

Although the Indus Valley civilization was completely destroyed, some of the key elements of the Harappan culture reappear in Indian art to this day. In contrast, the invading Aryans left almost no art at all. The literature of the time refers to elaborate wall paintings, woodcarving, jewellery making, metalwork, and also miniature painting. Nothing, however, survives today.

The only artefacts from that era which remain are copper tools and harpoons, and copper sheets with animals etched on them. There is also a new style of pottery called 'northern polished black ware' which emerged from the prevalent painted grey style around the middle of the 1st millennium.

However, the invading Aryans left several important legacies. One is the **caste system**, which is actually based on varna or colour. The defeated aboriginal peoples of the Indus Valley became a dark-skinned underclass of slaves and

A terracotta camel head from the Indus Valley

A typical terracotta, or baked earth, figurine of a 'mother goddess' from the Harappan culture

A terracotta pot unearthed at Kalibangan, made of kiln-fired clay and turned on an early potter's wheel

untouchables. Above them, with different degrees of racial mix, were the *shudras* or labourers, the *vaishyas* or merchants, the *kshatriyas* or warriors and, above all of them, the holy *brahmans* or priests.

The Aryans also brought with them the **Vedic religion**, which underlies three of the religions of India – Hinduism, Jainism and Buddhism. Vedism spawned a great explosion in literature, including the world's longest poem – the 90,000-verse *Mahabharata* – and the *Upanishads*. The principal book of Vedism, the *Rigveda,* was compiled between 1500 and 1000 BC and is the world's oldest religious text.

Vedism was slowly permeated by the beliefs of the indigenous people to form **Hinduism**. The Vedic literary tradition produced the *Vedanta*, meaning the end of the Vedas, and the *Brahma Sutras,* which are the origins of modern Hinduism. One of the important indigenous contributions which has its roots in pre-Aryan India was yoga, or the acquisition of knowledge through the control of the body. This was added to the two great Vedic paths to spiritual understanding – *jnana*, or the knowledge of the sacred texts, and *bhakti*, or love of the gods.

Jainism was founded in the 6th century BC when a monk named Mahavira, or Great Spirit, rejected the Vedic practice of animal sacrifice. Jainists are vegetarian and consider that to starve oneself to death is spiritually beneficial. Some even wear masks over their faces to prevent them from accidentally breathing in unseen microbes and they carry brooms to sweep tiny creatures out of their way when they walk. Their aim is to completely purify their minds and bodies and thus escape the endless cycle of death and rebirth.

About the same time Gautama (or Siddhartha), a prince of the Sakya republic in the foothills of Nepal, rejected the luxury and privilege of his birth. At the age of 29 he renounced the world, left his wife and child and sought a spiritual path. However, six years of austerity and self-mortification took him nowhere. But one day, sitting under a bodhi tree, he found his own way and soon became the **Buddha** – or the 'Enlightened One'. For the remaining 50 years of his life he travelled, while teaching the Four Noble Truths and the Noble Eightfold Path to Enlightenment.

The Four Noble Truths are: life is disappointment and suffering; suffering is caused by desire; to stop suffering you must overcome desire; and to overcome desire you must follow the Eightfold Path.

The elements of the Eightfold Path are: right views; right intentions; right speech; right conduct; right occupation – preferably being a monk; right effort; right awareness; and right meditation.

Thus, although the Aryan invasion destroyed India's earliest civilization, by underpinning three of its major religions the Aryans laid the foundation for the civilization that followed.

2 — THE FIRST IMPERIAL ART

he Aryans were not the only people to invade India. In the 5th century BC the Persian Empire began to encroach on the northwest. It brought with it the Aramaic script. At the same time a new civilization sprang up in Bihar and Uttar Pradesh.

In 326 BC **Alexander the Great** arrived. The young Macedonian had already conquered the eastern Mediterranean and the Persian Empire. Trying to consolidate his possessions, he crossed Afghanistan into Punjab with some 35,000 fighting men. There, with the help of the local ruler, Taxiles, he defeated Raja Porus's army of 50,000 troops and 200 elephants on the banks of the Jhelum river. This was Alexander's last great victory. With Porus now an ally, he marched eastwards. But his exhausted army refused to go on. So Alexander turned back, leaving India through Sind.

Even though he was in India for only a matter of months, Alexander left an impressive legacy. He founded two cities. One, Alexandria Nicaea, was established in order to celebrate his victory. The other, Bucephala, was named to commemorate his horse. One of Alexander's generals, Seleucus Nicator, was left behind to run these distant colonies.

A gold coin of ancient Greece, known as a stater, with the head of Alexander the Great, *circa* **323 BC**

Alexander's brief intervention nevertheless destabilized north India. A young warrior called **Chandragupta Maurya**, who had led a mounted band of irregular troops against Alexander, turned the situation to his advantage. He deposed the Nanda king at Pataliputra, near present-day Patna, and took over the kingdom of Magadha in the northeast. Then he turned against Seleucus Nicator who was forced to surrender the Greek possessions in India and much of Afghanistan in return for 500 elephants. However, Seleucus remained in control in Persia and established a treaty with the expanding **Mauryan Empire** through marriage. One of Seleucus's envoys, Megasthenes, visited Chandragupta's capital at Pataliputra and described it in his book *Indica*. The city stretched 9 miles (14 km) and was surrounded by a huge wooden wall with 64 gates and 570 towers. Chandragupta's palace, Megasthenes reported, outshone anything in Persia. This was a good comparison, since many of the artisans from the defeated Persian Empire came to the capital of the Mauryan Empire to find work. The fragments of Pataliputra so far unearthed show classic Persian modes of expression coupled with the Indian love of animals and nature. Towards the end of his life Chandragupta converted to Jainism and abdicated in favour of his son. He became a monk and travelled to south India where, in the Jainist way, he slowly starved himself to death.

The Great Stupa at Sanchi, in Madhya Pradesh, viewed from the south

Chandragupta's son Bindusara extended the Mauryan Empire as far south as Mysore. He was succeeded by the greatest of all the Mauryan emperors, **Asoka**, who further enlarged the empire with a bloody attack on Kalinga in 260 BC. About 150,000 people were captured; 100,000 were slaughtered and many more died as a result of the fighting.

Asoka was overcome with horror and regret at what he had done and immediately converted to Buddhism. He also sent out Buddhist missionaries into the rest of Asia and began a programme of stupa building to commemorate the Buddha's life. Stupas are dome-shaped mounds which usually conceal buried relics. Some of the more elaborate stupas have terraces and parasols and are decorated with bas-relief. Asoka was said to have built more than 80,000 of them.

The most famous was the **Great Stupa at Sanchi** in Madhya Pradesh, with a diameter of about 60 ft (18 m) and stood 25 ft (8 m) high. It had a walkway around it, 16 ft (5 m) above the ground, with a stairway leading up to it. A 9-ft (3-m) stone fence was built around the stupa and on the flattened top of the dome was a three-tiered parasol, inside a stone pen. The pen sprang from the tradition of enclosing sacred trees behind a fence and the three tiers of the parasol are supposed to symbolize the three jewels of Buddhism: the Buddha, the dharma or natural law and the fraternity of monks.

Asoka also built circular stone pillars marking places of special importance in the Buddha's life over an area stretching all the way from Delhi to Bihar. These are made of fine-grained sandstone, quarried at Chunar near Varanasi and fashioned in Asoka's imperial workshops. The monolithic pillars were erected without a base and taper gently towards the top. The capital usually carries a sculpted animal – perhaps an elephant or a bull, but most commonly a lion.

One of the best preserved pillars is the column at Lauriya Nandangartha in Bihar. It weighs a great 50 tons and stands 32 ft (10 m) high. Erecting it was a considerable feat of engineering. On the capital there is a seated lion.

The 7-ft (2-m) **Lion Capital from Sarnath** has been taken as the state emblem of modern India. It is, in fact, four identical lions joined back to back. Sarnath is, by tradition, the place where Buddha first started teaching his followers, and the lion is a symbol of the Buddha. It looks out to the four corners of the earth symbolized by the four animals beneath –

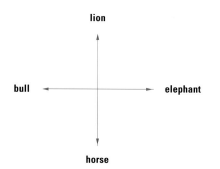

the bull to the west; the elephant to the east; the horse to the south; and the lion to the north. Between each animal is a wheel symbolizing the dharma. So the Lion Capital proclaims the Buddhist message out to the four corners of the world.

The work of Mauryan sculptors is characterized by the highly polished finish they give to their creations. This can be seen particularly on the near-perfect statue of a *yakshi*, or female earth spirit, found at Didarganj. She is portrayed life-size, carved from Chunar sandstone. Her full breasts and broad hips are reminiscent of the statuettes of 'mother goddesses' from the Indus Valley civilization, which had now come to represent the Indian ideal of female beauty. The same maternal qualities can be seen in the small ring stones from this period found all across northern India from Taxila, near the Khyber Pass, to Patna. These show a nude mother goddess in bas-relief and are plainly associated with some earth-mother cult.

The Mauryan gloss can also be seen on two small male torsos made in buff sandstone found at Lohanipur, which is again near Patna. These are the earliest known depictions of any of the 20 Jainist saints or *tirhankas*.

Two *yakshas*, or male earth-spirits, have been found from this period. One was discovered at Patna and, like the Didarganj yakshi, carries a fly whisk, which was a symbol of rank. It is life-size. The other, found at Parkham, near Mathura, is nearly 9 ft (3 m) tall and is executed in a much more primitive style. It has none of the rounded quality of the other statues. Instead, it is flattened, with little attention paid to the sides or back.

This is a style more commonly associated with woodcarving, although the Parkham yaksha is carved in a cream sandstone. At the same time artists were working in clay, and a large number of terracotta figurines have been found at Patna and across the plain of the Ganges. These are distinguished by their fine clothing and jewellery and the extremely sensitive rendering of their faces.

Buildings of this period were still constructed in wood and brick. None survive. However, a record of them is preserved in the rock-cut caves – a technique imported from Persia – which copy their form. The most important caves were in the Barabar and Nagarjuni Hills near Gaya in Bihar. Asoka had a series of chambers carved in the rock for the ascetics of the gloomy Ajivika sect, which sprang up round about the same time as Buddhism and Jainism. These monks would retreat to the chambers to meditate during the monsoon.

The Sudama and Lomas Rishi caves have long, barrel-vaulted halls, aping the wood construction of that period. In the Sudama cave there is also a stone facsimile of a circular wooden hut with a domed roof, carved to give the impression that it is thatched. The Lomas Rishi cave has an entrance way sculpted to look like a wooden portal. The stonemason has even carved a semicircular trellis above the doorway to let in light and air. Despite this effort to mimic wood and thatch, the interiors are burnished to give the Mauryan polish that so identifies this period.

The Lion Capital of the pillar erected by Asoka at Sarnath, *circa* **250 BC, now in the Archaeological Museum in Sarnath**

A detail from one of the magnificent carved stone Toranas, or gateways, which were added to the Great Stupa at Sanchi

A
soka ruled the Mauryan Empire for 37 years. When he died in 232 BC the empire was split between his son, Kunala, who ruled in the west from Gandhara, and his grandson, Dasartha, who ruled the eastern Magadha. This weakened the empire which shrank until it covered only the Ganges valley.

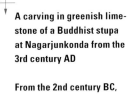

A carving in greenish lime- stone of a Buddhist stupa at Nagarjunkonda from the 3rd century AD

From the 2nd century BC, the red sandstone head of a Yakshi at Bharhut

Then, in 185 BC the last Mauryan emperor, Brhadratha, was killed by his Brahmin commander-in-chief, Pusyamitra, who founded the **Shunga dynasty** which lasted for 112 years. The Shungas changed the official religion of the empire to **Brahminism**. Despite the occasional persecution of Buddhists, the three principal religions continued to survive side by side. Buddhists, Jainists and Brahmins all constructed rock-cave retreats, often along the trade routes so that they could attract wealthy patrons.

The Buddhists carved a rock-cave prayer-hall or chaitya at Bhaja in the mid-2nd century BC. It has a barrel-vault roof, like the hall at Lomas Rishi, with two lines of free-standing pillars. At the back of the cave is a domed stupa and, on either side of the entrance, carved into the rock face were *viharas* – or monasteries – where the faithful lived in the small cells that surrounded the square communal halls.

These rock-cut chambers entailed an enormous amount of work. Hundreds of tons of rock had to be carved away with heavy iron picks. Then the sculptors would use chisels to finish the walls with religious reliefs.

The second great Shunga monument is also, ironically, Buddhist. It is the remains of the Bharhut stupa in Madhya Pradesh. In the Shunga era stupas had developed into hugely elaborate structures and, although the stupa itself has been removed completely by local people foraging for bricks, the stone wall and gateways that surround the stupa remain. Large reliefs carved into it illustrate the story of the Buddha's life and his previous incarnations. However, at this period the Buddha was never shown and his presence is represented by the Wheel of Dharma.

The everyday life of the court and common people was also depicted, along with pre-Buddhist earth-spirits. On one gatepost, Kubera, king of the *yakshas,* is portrayed. He is accompanied by Chandra, a *yakshi* depicted as a Shunga

The east gateway, one of the four such structures added to the Great Stupa at Sanchi by the Andhra

queen. Her leg brushes a tree trunk, showing that she is a *shalabhanjika* – a woman so beautiful and fertile that she can make a tree blossom with the merest touch of her foot.

Further development of the Shunga Empire was hampered by warfare. Its adversaries included the remnants of Alexander's Greeks, who clung on in Bactria, the Kalingas, who rebelled, the Scythians – or Shakas – and the Mongols from the steppes of Central Asia. Meanwhile, to the south, the **Andhra**, who had been a subject people under the Mauryan dynasty, rose to power. They renovated the **Great Stupa at Sanchi**, turning it into the finest Buddhist monument in the subcontinent. The Andhra's most glorious addition was four huge stone gates. These stood nearly 35 ft (11 m) high and were completed at the beginning of the Christian era. Each has two square gateposts, with sculpted animals or dwarfs on their capitals. They carry three architraves whose ends are spiralled like scrolls. These and the uprights supporting them are covered with reliefs. The crossbars also carry free-standing sculptures which, like the reliefs, depict scenes from the Buddha's early life, his previous incarnations and key scenes from early Buddhism – such as the visit of the Emperor Asoka to the bodhi tree where the Buddha found enlightenment. Animals, *yakshis* and *shalabhanjikas* are also depicted. But still the Buddha is nowhere to be seen. He is symbolized by a wheel, an empty throne and a pair of footprints. The figures are captured in movement and the whole composition is teeming with life. There is also a clue as to why this sculpture is so different from anything seen before. An inscription names one of the donors of the reliefs as the ivory workers of the nearby town of Vidishi. This could explain why the style is so rich, so fluid and so unlike the work of traditional stonemasons.

A mithuna couple at the entrance of the chaitya cave's central hall at Karli

The magnificent chaitya hall at Karli, near Bombay, from the 2nd century AD

Ivory carving from Andhra was greatly prized, even at the time. An ivory panel showing two women bedecked with jewels standing under a gateway, like that at Sanchi was found in Afghanistan and an ivory mirror-handle depicting a *yaksha* from this period was dug out of the ash at Pompeii.

The Andhra also built the Great Stupa at Amaravati, which was 162 ft (50 m) in diameter. It was covered in reliefs which were carved in green marble. Unfortunately it was destroyed in the 19th century. Many of the panels were consigned to a limekiln to make plaster. Those that remain are in the British and Madras Museums and are the prime examples of the flowering of what is known as the **Amaravati school**.

Many of the other great Buddhist monuments constructed by the Andhra have also perished. But the ***chaitya at Karli*** near Bombay has been preserved, again because it is a rock-cave. The main hall is 124 ft (38 m) long and 45 ft (14 m) high. At the far end is the stupa. The hall is flanked by two rows of decorative pillars which carry on their capital the sculpted figure of a royal personage mounted on a horse. Side doors are guarded by half life-size elephants which originally had ivory tusks and metal trappings.

On either side of the doorway to the central hallway are ***yakshas*** and ***yakshis*** who have by now evolved into noticeably amorous couples. This is the beginning of the mithuna or erotic tradition in Indian temple carving.

As the Amaravati school of sculpture developed the figures became slimmer, more elongated and more graceful. Then, suddenly, at the end of the 2nd century AD, depictions of the Buddha appeared. A circular relief from the railings of the Great Stupa, which were added at the beginning of the 3rd century AD, shows the Buddha in human form pacifying an enraged elephant sent by an envious relative. At the time there was a great movement of Buddhist monks coming out of the monasteries and into the community, and they needed some sort of image to carry with them.

The Yueh-Chih tribes from Mongolia had subdued much of Central Asia at the beginning of the Christian era. During the

2nd century BC they invaded Bactria and eventually dominated all northeast India down as far as Sanchi. They adopted the Greek alphabet and, by the first century AD, had unified to form the **Kushan nation**, which was ruled from Kabul. The Kushan started trading with the Romans down the Silk Road and began striking their own gold coins. They had adopted Persian fire worship, but their coins carried images of Greek, Roman, Brahmin and Persian gods – along with an image of the standing Buddha. Sometimes he was portrayed with a halo. His earlobes were extended by heavy earrings and his right hand was sometimes raised as a blessing. Around the end of the 1st century AD the Kushan king Kanishka converted to Buddhism and consequently spread the faith throughout Central Asia and China. The Kushans employed Roman and Greek sculptors to produce new images of the Buddha. They copied the early characteristics of the Buddha seen on the coins in stone. Then, in a frieze depicting the four stages of the Buddha's life made in Gandhara in the 2nd century AD, he is shown in the lotus position – now all the classic elements of the image of Buddha had at last come together.

A 55 meter high Buddha, at Bamiyan in Afghanistan, carved in the rocks by monks and defaced over the years

Buddhist monks flocked north to Gandhara where the Kushans built huge monasteries and stupas. There were vast galleries of sculptures of Buddha and **bodhisattvas** – Buddhist saints who were capable of enlightenment. Stupas became larger and taller. The stupa at Peshawar rose 700 ft (213 m) from a plinth 300 ft (90 m) in diameter and was topped with a 13-tier golden parasol. However, the **Gandhara school** did not confine itself to Buddhist imagery. The Hindu deities Indra and Brahma were also depicted and influences from Persia and Rome are discernible.

In the middle of the 3rd century AD the Sassanians overthrew the Parthians in Persia and all trade along the Silk Road came to a complete halt. This considerably weakened the great Kushan Empire and in the 5th century Gandhara was totally overrun by the White Huns.

There was a second centre of artistic activity in the Kushan Empire, at Mathuri, which is some 8 miles (13 km) to the south of Delhi on the Jumna river. Nearby, at Mat, a shrine was built to the Kushan dynasty. Huge figures of King Vima Kadphises and his successor, King Kanishka, were housed there. Other sculptures of Kushan princes carved in the distinct local red sandstone were found in shrines nearby.

A large number of voluptuous *yakshis* were also discovered in
the area, suggesting that the cult of the mother goddess still
flourished. But, under the thrall of Buddhism, these were
slowly transformed into bodhisattva figures. The masterpiece of the
Mathura school is a Buddha seated on a lion throne
in red sandstone. He is depicted in the
lotus position with his right hand raised in benediction.
However, unlike the Buddhas from Gandhara, this sculpture
betrays no Greek or Roman influence. At the time the
Mathuran workshops were exporting their work to Sarnath
and to Buddha's homeland of Doab. The Mathuran Buddha is
the prototype for the figure now seen throughout the East.

**A seated bodhisattva,
carved in red sandstone at
Mathura, 1st century AD**

**A bodhisattva from
Shabbaz Garhi in the
Gupta style**

nder the Gupta Empire, which arose in Bihar around AD 320, there was an outpouring of science, literature, music and the visual arts. The empire spread across northern India and lasted over 200 years. It is seen as India's classical age.

The red sandstone figure of a standing Buddha, Jamalpur, Mathura, 5th century AD

A buff sandstone head of the Buddha, also dating from the 5th century AD and found at Sarnath

Before achieving power the Guptas were almost unknown. Originally from eastern Uttar Pradesh, the third king, Chandra Gupta I, extended his rule to Magadha by marrying a Licchavi princess, an event celebrated in a series of gold coins. He was the first of the dynasty to take the title *maharajadhiraja* (supreme king). His son, Samdra Gupta, and his grandson, Chandra Gupta II, spread the empire west and southwards with a series of conquests and marriages.

During this period of expansion the Guptas took over the workshops at Mathura. Classical Gupta style is derived from Kushan style, but the Guptas later tried consciously to emulate the Mauryans. They even moved their seat of government from Prayaga – now Allahabad – in Uttar Pradesh to the Mauryan capital of Pataliputra, near Patna.

The golden age of Gupta art was during the reign of Chandra Gupta II (380–415). In this period the craftsmen of Mathura

produced the great **Standing Buddha** which is now in the National Museum, New Delhi. Carved from red sandstone, it is executed in the monumental style of the Mauryans. But there are Kushan touches, especially in the gown which is so delicately sculpted that it appears almost transparent. The sheer fabric is defined only by an arrangement of delicate folds. This way of portraying fabric becomes even more refined in a series of so-called **'wet Buddhas'** unearthed at Sarnath. The cloth clings so tightly to the body that it looks as if the statues have been dowsed with water. One of these wet Buddhas shows a seated Buddha teaching the law. His robe is indicated only by lines around his neck, wrists and ankles, and a small ruff under his crossed feet. The simplicity of the figure contrasts with the elaborate patterns in his halo, in which artists of this period indulged their love of decoration.

The right hand is raised up, in the now familiar open-palmed gesture known as the *dharma chakra mudra*. This image has moved on from the Buddha on the lion throne, characteristic of the Kushan period. The Buddha now has a serene look on his face, with his eyes cast down, averted from the world as if in meditation. **Bronze Buddhas** also from this period have been recovered. These also have the Mathuran 'wet look'. Coloured relief images of the Buddha discovered at Mirpur Khas reveal a slenderness and delicacy that harks back to Gandhara. Moreover, the small ivory Buddhas from Kashmir survived in the mountain monasteries.

During the Gupta period a large number of terracotta decorated stupas were built. But Hinduism was now in the ascendancy. Many temples and shrines to Hindu gods were erected and the craftsmen of Mathura produced a large number of images of Hindu divinities, especially of **Vishnu-Krishna**.

A Gupta period bronze Buddha, 6th century AD

Opposite, a buff sandstone carving of the Buddha in the attitude of preaching a sermon, from Sarnath

A painting illustrating the
Miracle of Sravast from the
fabulous caves of Ajanta

A painted Buddha with
attendants, from Cave 17
at Ajanta, Maharashtra,
circa 5th / 6th century AD

One of the finest is the famous image of Vishnu wearing a crown and regal jewellery in the National Museum, New Delhi. During the reign of Chandra Gupta II a Hindu rock-cut shrine was carved out in Udayagiri, near Vidisha. In it there are a series of sculptures and reliefs, fashioned in soft stone. The most magnificent shows Vishna rescuing the beautiful earth goddess from a demon serpent who has dragged her down into the watery depths. Vishna is incarnated as a man with a boar's head. He carries the goddess easily on his shoulder and is attended by a crowd of lesser gods and human beings who all celebrate his triumph. This relief is pure Gupta but does also contains many Kushan elements.

Kushan *yakshis* were undergoing a transition at Udayagiri. They abandoned their trees for water and at the Gupta shrine at Beshagar the *yakshi* is transformed into the river goddess Ganga, standing on a *makara,* which is half-crocodile and half-elephant. Another *yakshi* can be seen standing on the back of a tortoise, which represents the sacred Jumna river.

The Siva temples at Bhumara and Nachna Kuthara also contain sculpture of extraordinary precision and skill. Particular care has been lavished on the decorative elements, especially large reliefs covered with lotus stems and flower-strewn scrolls.

Some of the finest sculpture of this period can be seen on the walls of the temple of Vishnu at Deogarh. The door frame of the sanctum is covered with figures of worshippers, angels, floral scrolls and amorous couples – all typical motifs of the period. There are also three large relief panels, showing the penance of Nara-Narayana, the rescue of an elephant and Vishnu asleep on the many-headed serpent, Ananta. These echo much of the Buddhist style seen at Sarnath.

The Vakataka dynasty had taken over from the Andhras in central India. They secured an alliance with the Guptas through marriage. Many of the artistic ideas generated in the north found expression here, too. Massive sculptures adorned the rock-cave temple of Shiva at Elephanta, an island about 6 miles (10 km) offshore in Bombay harbour, and the Buddhist *chaitya* and *viyana* caves at **Ajanta**. Work there began in the 2nd century BC and continued for 300 years. In all, 29 caves were carved out of a cliff around a horseshoe-shaped ravine. They were then lost until the early 19th century when they were rediscovered by a party out hunting tigers.

Not only are the caves at Ajanta full of reliefs, decorative wall carvings and sculptures, but they also contain the oldest surviving examples of **Indian painting.** The earliest comes from the 1st century BC. It is badly fragmented, but enough remains to see that it depicts a royal procession. The quality of the painting also shows that this was by no means the beginning of work in this medium. A long tradition of painting had gone before which is now, unfortunately, lost.

The paintings were executed on a carefully prepared surface. A thick layer of potter's clay mixed with straw, animal hair and dung was spread on the rock wall and levelled off. This was coated with fine white plaster. While this was still damp, the painting was outlined in red. The areas in between were then given an undercoat of grey or green earth and the shapes filled in with colours. A brown or black outline was then added to the figures and the finished painting was burnished with a smooth stone until it shone.

The walls were covered mostly with religious paintings, showing the lives and incarnations of Buddha and various bodhisattvas,

The Chaitya Hall (Buddhist
prayer hall) from Cave 19 in
the Ajanta caves, in which
the abundance of images
reflects Mahayan Buddhist
art at its most magnificent

while the ceilings were decorated with animals, plants, and other things taken from nature. Elephants, horses, bulls, birds, monkeys and the ladies of the court are also woven into the stories told on the walls. Some figures echo the depiction of *yakshas* and *yakshis.* There are also illustrations of ancient myths, some with erotic overtones.

Just as the White Huns – or Hunas – had destroyed the Kushan Empire, they gradually overran the Gupta Empire, too. A new empire emerged in northern India under King Harsa, who was also the subject of the first major biography in Sanskrit. He was a writer himself, the author of three noted Sanskrit plays, and he made his capital Kannauj a haven for the arts. However, his attempt to invade the Chalukya kingdom to the south failed.

In the 5th century the Chalukya had built some of the earliest Hindu temples. These were based on early Buddhist shrines but, like the Ladkhan temple at Aihole, they contained a stone phallus representing the god Shiva rather than an image of the Buddha. A second temple at Aihole, built about 100 years later, has some wonderful examples of Chalukyan sculpture. More can be seen at Badami, where the Chalukya established their capital. Above the town, four pillared halls are carved into the cliffs – one dedicated to Shiva and two to Vishnu, the fourth being a Jainist shrine. The earliest of the Vaishnava halls, which is dedicated to Vishnu, was completed around 580. It contains a huge statue of Vishnu, seated on the serpent Ananta, whose hoods fan out above his head like a halo. The verandah was painted, but little remains. The Chalukyas also built a huge free-standing temple to the north of Badami.

In the mid-8th century the Chalukyas were replaced by the Rashtrakuta dynasty. Their second king, Krishna I, built the great rock-cut **Kailasanatha Temple** at Elura in Maharashtra. Elura had long been a place of pilgrimage for Buddhists, Hindus and Jains, who each had numerous shrines carved into the rock there.

Krishna I had some three million cubic ft (84,000 cubic m) of rock removed to sculpt the four main chambers of the temple into the mountainside. The shrine to Nandi, the bull on which

A massive elephant and column in the Kailasanatha Temple of Shiva at Elura

The awesome main hall of the Temple, which is borne on the backs of elephants gathering lotuses

The triple-headed Shiva Mahesamurti, or Trimurti, of Elephanta. On the left is the wrathful Bhairava, on the right the sublime Vamadeva, spirit of the creation, and centre the Great God Shiva Mahadeva

Shiva rides, is flanked by two 60-ft (18-m) free-standing pillars and two huge life-size stone elephants. The tower of the inner sanctum that contains the phallus symbol of Shiva rises up to nearly 100 ft (30 m) and is carried on the backs of many ranks of carved elephants.

This temple complex is situated in a courtyard 154 ft (47 m) wide by 276 ft (84 m) deep, which is surrounded by a rock wall 120 ft (37 m) high. The huge temple itself is covered in the finest examples of Rashtrakuta sculpture and smaller shrines are carved in its walls. The name Kailasanatha means 'Lord Shiva's mountain home' – it is the Hindu equivalent of Mount Olympus – and the temple teems with gods, demons and even mere mortals.

The Rashtrakutas sculpted another rock-carved temple to Shiva at Elephanta. It has a floor space of more than 16,000 sq ft (1,440 sq m). In the porch and the main hall there are seven huge reliefs showing scenes from the story of Shiva. Giant figures flank the doorways to the phallus shrine.

Sadly, many of these treasures were destroyed by the Portuguese who installed a military garrison on Elephanta, using the temple of Shiva as a shooting gallery. Incredibly, though, an 18-ft (5-m) high **statue of Shiva** came through unscathed. This three-headed sculpture in brown sandstone is one of the most famous images of the god. One face shows him as the creator, soft and feminine with pearls and flowers in his hair and a lotus in his hand. Another shows him as destroyer, angry and cruel, with a hooked nose and the death's head adorning his head-dress. The central face shows him as the all-powerful god, as serene and unworldly as the Buddha.

5 — SOUTH INDIA

To the south of the Chalukyas were the Pallavas who had occupied southeast-India from the 1st century BC. They were a trading nation and their principal city was the port of **Mamallapuram** – now Mahabalipuram – some 40 m (65 km) from Madras. In the 5th century AD the Pallavas converted from Buddhism to Brahminism and in the 7th century Mamallapuram became a centre of the arts.

In the late 7th–early 8th centuries a huge relief showing the descent of the sacred river Ganges was carved there. It is 80 ft (24 m) long and 20 ft (6 m) high. The relief depicts the king and queen of the serpents swimming up the stream as it falls from heaven. To the left is the ascetic Bhagiratha, whose 1,000 years of self-denial persuaded the gods to bestow the Ganges on the world. To the right is a huge elephant. Shiva and his female incarnation, Durga, also appear. All the figures have a distinctive slenderness and grace.

At the south of Mamallapuram are five free-standing carved temples, or **raths**. *Rath* means 'chariot' and the temples were meant to be the vehicles of the gods. They are mounted on carved wheels, four of them sculpted from a single block of granite. The walls and roofs, which are carved to resemble wooden structures, teem with reliefs and sculpted statues. Between *raths* there are statues of bulls, lions and elephants.

The magnificent Shore Temple at Mamallapuram. Built during the early 8th century AD, it represents the earliest example of a stone-built temple in the south of India

In the 8th century the Shore Temple, dedicated to Shiva, was constructed on the sea front at Mamallapuram. The temple was constructed out of granite blocks, rather than carved from rock already in place and was the first stone-built temple in southern India. It had two huge towers and the building was covered with reliefs and carvings, although most of these have been largely eroded.

Further to the south were the **Cholas**, who overran the Pallavas at the end of the 9th century. They also expanded their empire to the south, ejecting the Pandyas from southern India and invading Sri Lanka. By the end of the 10th century they were strong enough to challenge the Chalukyas, who had re-emerged as a force in the north.

To celebrate his victory over the Chalukyas the Chola king, Rajara I, built a massive temple to Shiva in his capital, Tanjore. Known as the **Rajarajeshvara Temple**, it features a huge pyramid, sitting on top of an 82-ft (25-m) square base and rising to some 190 ft (58 m). On the top is a domed capstone weighing about 80 tons.

Chola stonemasons created other masterpieces. The most notable are: the relief at Gangaikondacholapuram showing Shiva bestowing a victory garland on Rajendra Chola, who had conquered Sumatra and Bengal; the four-headed Brahmani at Kanchipuram; and Shiva the Great Teacher, who is depicted crushing ignorance, symbolized by a dwarf, under his foot. However, Chola artists were even more renowned for their use of bronze. The tradition of using bronze as a sculptural medium was transmitted via the Andhras, through the Pallavas, to the

A masterpiece of southern Indian architecture, the Rajarajeshvara Temple at Tanjore is dominated by the pyramid tower over the Nandi shrine, seen here in the background to the left.

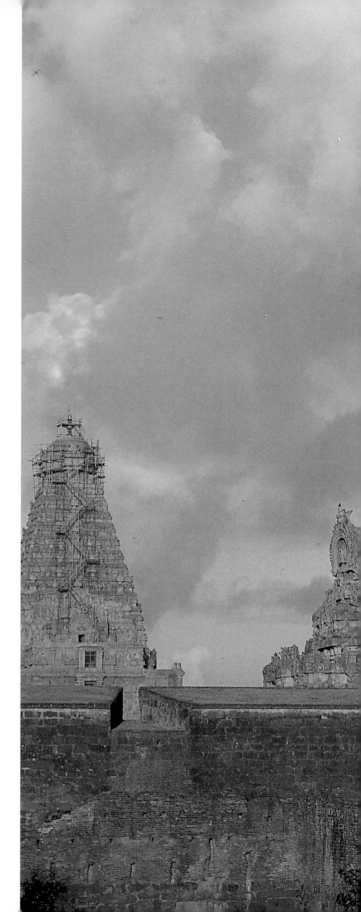

Cholas. Like the Harappans they used the lost-wax process. Many Hindu bronzes look alike, not because they were cast – the clay mould would be destroyed in the process – but because the image was precisely specified by religious canon. Much of Chola bronze work concentrates on Shiva in his many incarnations and his consort Parvati. But the Chola bronze-smiths eschew the voluptuous depiction of the traditional female form, favouring a more slender and graceful figure. The greatest icon among the Chola bronzes is **Shiva as Lord of the Dance**. He is depicted with his hair flying. His legs and his four arms are full of movement. He is ringed with flames, symbolizing the firmament.

In the mid-13th century the **Hoysalas** rose to power in the area around Mysore. They built a series of temples whose intricate decoration completely obscured the architectural structure. This was achieved by carving the elaborate reliefs in soft soapstone, which hardened with prolonged exposure to air. The most famous example is the complex of the three star-shaped **shrines to Vishnu at Somnathpur**. They stand on a huge plinth in a walled compound.

The best known example of Hoysala sculpture is the elaborate relief showing the Lord **Ganesha**, Shiva's elephant-headed son, now in the Asian Art Museum in San Francisco. The image is frequently seen in business premises in India. Hindus believe, that when properly propitiated, Ganesha is supposed to help overcome all obstacles.

The last great temple builders of south India were the Nayak dynasty, who created the Great Temple at Madurai in the 17th century. In fact, it is huge temple complex, surrounding a ritual bathing pool. The largest of the temples is the Hall of the Thousand Pillars, but the most extraordinary feature of the temple city is the towering gateways, whose many tiers are a complex frenzy of sculpture.

A Chola bronze of Chandra, god of the moon, and Soma, who merged to make one

Part of the soapstone relief on one of the star-shaped sanctuaries of the Keshava Temple in Somanthpur

Shiva, Lord of the Dance, surrounded by the flames of the firmament

Ganesha, son of Shiva, in a fine-grained chloritic schist from the Hoysala period in Mysore

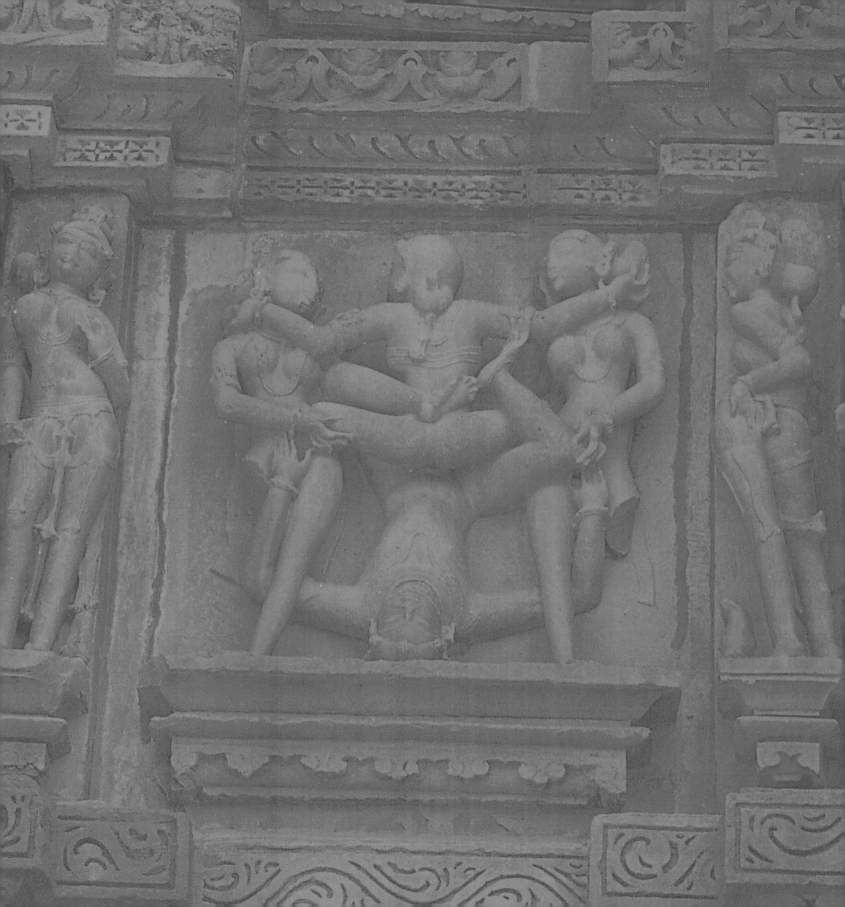

n the 8th century
India was divided.
In the north rival
states squabbled,
while Islam gained
strength in the wings. Then, in 712, the Arabs
invaded Sind. However, the story of Buddhism
in India still had a few centuries to run.

The round stone gateway
to the Mukteshvara Temple
(950 AD), an example of the
Orissan style found in the
Bhuvaneshvar region

The Mahabodhi Temple at
Bodh Gaya, built in the 7th
and 8th century AD

At Bodh Gaya the huge **Mahabodi Temple** was built.
Its pyramidal tower, rising to 180 ft (55 m), was a radical
departure from the small shrines on the site up to that time
and echoes the monumental Hindu temples built in the south.
New stupas were erected in the university city of Nalanda. The
relief patterns that decorated them owe much to the work of
the Gupta period. The craftsmen of Nalanda also began to
produce work in bronze.

At the time Buddhism was coming under the influence of
Tantric Hinduism and Buddhist art borrowed obscure Tantric
symbols that could be deciphered only by the initiated. The
bodhisattvas (Buddhas in waiting) became gods. Their images
– particularly those of Padmapani, or 'he who holds the lotus',
and Avalokiteshvara, 'the god who looks down' – proliferated
and the simplified style inherited from the Guptas gradually
became overlaid with elaborate ornamentation. By the time of

the 10th century, in Bihar, the Buddha, who had once been an ascetic, appeared wearing a crown and bedecked with jewels. Craftsmen had recycled the image of Buddha so often that it became cold and stereotyped. Moreover, the influence of the surrounding Hindu community grew so strong that the Buddha began to look like a Hindu god. Indeed, by the 12th century, Hindus were beginning to accept the Buddha as the ninth incarnation of Vishnu and the two religious and artistic traditions began to converge.

Images of Vishnu that had formerly been executed in stone now appeared in bronze. The technique of casting meant that more elaborate detail could be incorporated, even on a smaller scale. Precious metals were inlaid in the bronze and some smaller figures were cast in silver and gold.

There were also developments in temple building in northern India. Small towers had already been added to the flat-roofed temples at Aihole and Bahami in central India. In the mid-8th century the Parasurameshvara Temple at Bhuvaneshar was built with a huge tower as its central feature. It was built over a square assembly hall. The walls arched gently inwards as it rose and it was capped with a flat, circular stone. This style was copied and developed in other temples on the same site over the next 300 years.

Medieval temples were built following the rules laid down in ancient manuals called **Shastras**. Mortar was rarely used

One of the wheels of the sun god's chariot carved around the base of the Black Pagoda, or Surya Temple, at Konarak

and the buildings were held together simply by their own weight and bulk. The hugely ornate exteriors were carved with the stone *in situ*.

The **Black Pagoda at Konarak** is considered to be one of the great masterpieces of the medieval era, even though it was never completed. But the Surya Temple, as it is more properly called, was built on the edge of the beach of the Bay of Bengal and the sandy foundations would never have been able to support the weight of its tower, which would have stood well over 200 ft (60 m) high.

The temple is supposed to represent the sun god's chariot. There are wheels carved around the base and it is pulled by seven stone horses.

It may well have been a centre for a Tantric cult, since the walls are covered with erotic carvings showing couples engaged in all manner of sexual acts.

Female musicians entertain the sun god and the dancers depicted resemble ancient *yakshis*. Inside, a life-size figure of the god Surya in green chlorite competes with two images of Rajah Narasimhadeva I who built the temple. Surya is shown

in Guptan simplicity, while the sculptor records every little detail of Narasimhadeva's opulence.

The **temples of Khajuraho** – the 'city of the Gods' – built between 950 and 1050 also escaped the attentions of the Islamic invaders. The Muslims destroyed many temples. To them the depiction of human and animal forms was a sacrilege and they were particularly offended by the Tantric carvings. Khajuraho was never invaded and its huge temples seethe with layer upon layer of human life.

Many of its sculptures are highly erotic. Even the nymphs and temple dancers are lithe and full-breasted.

At the time the Muslims were invading, the Jains brought medieval sculpture and architecture in western India to their finest flowering at the temple complex on the 4,000-ft (1,200-m) peak of the sacred mountain, **Mount Abu**. The Vimala Sha Temple, completed in 1032, was carved from white marble. The statues which decorated it were brought from many hundreds of miles away. Many of the images in this Jainist temple are borrowed from the dominant Hindu culture, but the new religion sweeping across northern India would not be so tolerant of other faiths.

Opposite, the Sassoon Dillawara Temple, part of the temple complex upon Mount Abu

An erotic figure from the Parsvanatha Temple at Khajuraho, 'city of the Gods'

7 — ISLAMIC ART

Arab traders had occupied Sind since the 8th century, but wholesale conquest did not begin until the 11th century when Mahmud of Ghazna made more than 20 raids into northern India from Afghanistan and eventually annexed Punjab.

Although his empire may have been short-lived, he paved the way by revealing to the Muslim world the wealth of India and demonstrating that the subcontinent was vulnerable to attack. Turks and Persians struggled for power, but it was another Afghan, Muhammad of Ghur, who, after a number of setbacks, swept across northern India. Delhi fell in 1193. Muhammad's viceroy, Qutb-ud-Din Aybak, established his capital there. To celebrate Islam's victory over Hinduism, he built the **Quwat-ul-Islam** – or 'Might of Islam' – mosque on the site of Delhi's largest temple. Completed in 1196, it was constructed out of masonry from the Hindu and Jainist shrines he had destroyed. Outside the mosque stood the Qutb Minar, a 288-ft (88-m) minaret, designed to cast the shadow of Allah over the inhabitants of Delhi.

In order to build the mosque Qutb-ud-Din employed Hindu craftsmen and they incorporated Indian emblems into the

Tombs of the Tughluq dynasty outside Delhi

The imposing Man Madir Palace at Gwalior, Madhya Pradesh, completed in 1516

design. The minaret has bands of quotations from the holy Koran carved in it, and between them are strips of Indian floral decorations. The arched facade, added in 1198, was designed to give the mosque an Arabic appearance, but it was built using many Indian techniques and is therefore covered with Indian ornamentation. So, from the early days of the Islamic invasion, a hybrid style was developing.

In the 14th century the Tughluq dynasty brought the Afghan style to Delhi. Their monumental buildings are made from coarse rubble overlaid with plaster. They were quite simple and carried little decorations. But ornamentation returned to Delhi with the Lodi sultanate (1479–1526) which introduced a more opulent, Persian style to the city. Typical of this style is the **Tomb of Isa Khan** completed in 1547. It has the thick walls and low dome that would be influential on design long into the reign of the Mughals.

Outside Delhi the provinces became independent sultanates and started to strike out on their own architecturally. The Adina mosque was built at Pandua in Bengal between 1364 and 1369 from the remains of Indian temples. In the 15th century the Sharqi dynasty in Uttar Pradesh built a series of mosques at Jaunpur. These are unique because of their huge *maqsurahs* or gateways that are so large that they completely obscure the domes of the temples.

The Hindu kingdoms to the south also flourished during this period. Between 1430 and 1469 Rana Kumbha built a series of palaces at Chitor, now in ruins, and the magnificent **Man Mandir** palace at Gwalior was completed in 1516. Indo-Islamic culture reached new heights with the **Mughal Empire**. The first Mughal ruler was Babur, a descendant of both Tamerlane, the Turk who invaded India in 1398, and of

Genghis Khan. Hence, he was called the Mughal, or Mongol. Babur was crowned king of Farghana, now part of Uzbekistan, at the age of 11, but was deposed. For the next 20 years he had to fight for his birthright and sharply honed his military skills in the process.

He never regained his kingdom in Central Asia, and turned his attention instead to Punjab. He used that as a base to attack Delhi, which he took in 1526. By the time he died in 1530 he had extended his empire across most of northern India.

Babur's son Humayun was the first real Mughal emperor, but his empire had yet to be consolidated: his treasury was empty and there were disputes among his family. Although Humayun's name means 'fortunate', he was anything but that. After a series of disastrous military and political moves, he was driven from India in 1540 by Sher Shah, an Afghan rebel from Bihar and forced to seek refuge in Persia.

But then his luck began to change. When Sher Shah died in 1553, the country collapsed into civil war and Humayun managed to retrieve his throne. In Persia he had been much impressed with that country's miniature painting and, when he returned to Delhi in 1555, he brought with him two Persian artists, Abdus Samad and Mir Sayyid.

Humayun died a year after regaining his throne. His beautiful **tomb in Delhi** was built by his widow in red sandstone inlaid with white marble. Designed in a mixed Persian and Indian style, it was to be the model for the great Taj Mahal.

The celebrated red sandstone
Tomb of Humayun in Delhi,
(1565), which is thought to be
the model for the Taj Mahal

Fatehpur Sikri, a perfectly
preserved Moghul city
built by Akbar the Great
(1571-86) as his capital

A marble grill in the Tomb
of Salim Chistri, to be
found in Fatehpur Sikri

The Mughals were not very strict Muslims and they quickly dispensed with any of the trappings of the Islamic state.

Humayun's successor, Akbar the Great, founded a new religion called Din-i-Illali, and insisted on giving all his Hindu and Muslim subjects equal rights.

Akbar was also interested in architecture. After a Muslim holy man had correctly predicted the birth of his son, Akbar decided to build a new royal city called **Fatehpur Sikri** on the site of the hermit's hideaway, about 30 miles (48 km) from Agra. The project began in 1571 and hundreds of labourers were employed to build a city 2 miles (3.2 km) long by a mile (1. 6 km) wide. There were mosques, palaces, tombs, formal courtyards, ceremonial buildings, harems, reflecting pools – everything except water. So when after 15 years the city was completed, sadly, it had to be abandoned.

During Humayun's exile Akbar had learnt to draw and, under the tutorship of Abdus Samad and Mir Sayyid, he established the **Mughal School of Indian painting**. About 100 artists, mainly Hindu, studied there.

Its first major production was the *Dastan i-Amir Hamaza* (The Romance of Amir Hamaza). It is a series of 2-ft (60-cm) high, beautiful paintings on cloth with writing on the back, so that the story could be read while the paintings were displayed at court. Altogether there were 1,400 paintings, collected in 12 volumes. They were executed in a distinctive Akbari style, which mixed Persian and Indian elements, and their use of space and action proved to be highly influential.

In 1578 a new element was added. Portuguese missionaries from Goa had brought Akbar illustrated Bibles and religious pictures. Always enthusiastic about the arts, he was much taken with the European style and ordered his painters to study them. Mughal artists were soon introducing realism and perspective. Some miniaturists even painted Christian subjects, complete with cherubs and golden haloes.

Paper replaced cloth as the base medium for miniatures. It was burnished first and the outline was sketched in red ink. Once the artist had corrected it, the amended outline was traced in black. A thin wash of white pigment was laid down as a base for the gouache. Any gold was then added and the finished painting was burnished again.

A miniature featuring the Mughal emperor Jahangir holding court

The most famous of all Indian buildings, a symbol of the sub-continent, the fabulous Taj Mahal

When Akbar died in 1605 his son Jahangir was his successor. He was also a painting enthusiast and prided himself on his ability to recognize the work of individual artists. He was interested in natural history and sent painters out to record the flora and fauna of his empire. They were also instructed to record life at the court. Sadly, as a result their work depicted Jahangir's slow decline into opium addiction.

After Jahangir's death in 1627 Mughal painting itself went into decline. The artists had so perfected their technique that their output became cold and lifeless. Jahangir's son and successor, Shah Jahan, was in any case more interested in architecture. Early in his reign buildings constructed in white marble began to appear across the empire and when his beloved queen Mumtaz died, he built her a huge white marble mausoleum at Agra – the justly famous **Taj Mahal**. Its white marble walls are subtly accentuated with delicate patterns of black stone and the dome is raised on a cylinder similar to that on Tamerlane's tomb in Samarkand.

Shah Jahan also added the marble Pearl Mosque to the Red Fort at Agra. He built a second **Red Fort** in Old Delhi, the new royal city which he laid out. Italian workmen were brought in to produce the mosaic work in its white marble pavilions. Shah Jahan's son, Aurangzeb, was a bird of a different feather. He deposed his father and reimposed strict Islamic law. He also withdrew his patronage from the arts and the Hindu artists of the Mughal school left Delhi to find work. When Aurangzeb died in 1707 his empire shrank to the area around Delhi. But all was not lost. By the time his great-grandson, Muhammad Shah, came to the throne in 1719, there were still enough artists from the Mughal School to stage an artistic revival. This was distinguished by its detailed depiction of nature and the romantic treatment of young lovers.

Painting was also developing fast in the Islamic kingdoms of central India. The earliest known **Deccan miniatures** were produced to illustrate the *Tarif i-Husayn Shahi.* This was a Persian-style epic that celebrated the life of Husayn Nizam Shahi I, the ruler of Ahmadnagar and it was commissioned by his queen. People were portrayed as tall and thin, with elongated faces.

Painting from the Deccan developed a new elegance and refinement.

Colour was applied more delicately. Some Hindu influences were also absorbed, along with those from outside India, since trading by sea with the subcontinent was flourishing. However, like Jahangir, the Deccan artists' greatest patron, Ibrahim Adil Shah II, the ruler of Bijapur, died in 1627 and sadly, Deccan painting went into decline.

A late example of a Deccan miniature from Bijapur, a portrait of Ali Adil Shah *circa* 1680

Sikhs at the Delhi Gate in the Red Fort, Old Delhi

8 — THE RISE OF PAINTING

painting in India began as small illustrations in palm-leaf books around the start of the Christian era. Unfortunately, none survive. The oldest Indian paintings still in existence come from the 11th century.

A Jainist miniature from Gujarat, 'The Consecration of Mahavira'

Miniatures in the style of the Rajasthani school often featured the romance of Krishna and Radha

Early Buddhist works from Bengal and Bihar were largely destroyed during the rise of Islam, although some notable examples escaped. The works of **Jainist artists** in Gujarat got off more lightly, since the artists were protected by their rich patrons.

The distinctive characteristic of early Jainist paintings is that, although faces are depicted in profile, both eyes are shown. The eye that would normally be invisible hovers over the bridge of the nose.

Paper, which came to India from Persia, had all but replaced palm leaf by 1400. This gave Indian artists a larger area to work with and a Persian influence took hold. Jainist icons were replaced by images from nature and architecture. The Persian vertical style and the Jainist two-eyed depiction of profile spread across northern India. Narratives also became important. One prime example of the illustrated narrative from

The celebrated 'Raja Umed
Singh of Kotah Shooting
Tiger' *circa* 1780

A Sikh painting dating
from 1830-40 entitled
'Sikh Prince Hunting'

15th-century Uttar Pradesh is the romance *Laur Chanda*.

In the 16th century the palette brightened. Greens and blues were added to the reds, yellows, golds, blacks and whites. Blue also replaced the traditional red background.

The Muslim invasion of India destroyed the ancient Sanskrit tradition and a new native Hindu literature grew up, illustrated in the lively **Rajasthani style**. Images of Krishna and Radha, the lovers of Hindu myth, were used to illustrate more secular love stories. Although it employs many of the realistic techniques of Mughal art, Rajasthani painting is largely symbolic. For example, if there are a number of women in a painting, they are all copies of one another. When painting a woman the Rajasthani artist is not trying to depict any one particular woman; rather he is attempting to reveal the essence of all womanhood through that single figure.

Rajasthani miniature paintings were part of a comprehensive theory of art. Each colour was related to a particular musical note and had specific meaning. Brown was considered erotic, red denoted rage and yellow the fabulous. This led to the school of miniature painting known as the *ragamala*, where paintings are related to raga music, an improvised style that is concerned primarily with the emotions. In painting the emotions were revealed by areas of bright colours broken up by images from folk art.

By the early 17th century western Indian features had totally disappeared and the areas of colour became more fragmented. They were, however, still flat, with no attempt at shading or modelling, and trees and figures were elongated to fit better into the vertical format.

Shadows and more subtle coloration were added by the artists of Bundi state, under the influence of the school of Shah

Jahan. Around 1780 the nearby state of Kotah provided the incomparable ***Raja Umed Singh of Kotah Shooting Tiger***. It displays a cruder and more decorative style. Another vibrant regional style grew up in Kishangarth, just 60 miles (96 km) from Bundi, in the court of the Raja Savant Singh, who was also a noted poet. Love became the most dominant theme of **Rajput art**. The paintings often reflected extremely passionate feelings and were also full of highly erotic symbolism.

In the foothills of the Himalayas yet another style developed. It was the product of the Mughal artists who left Delhi during the periodic reassertion of Islamic principles. The Pahari style, which began in Basohli, is distinctive in its combative profiles and bold use of colour. Fragments of beetles' wings were often incorporated in order to make jewellery shine. Its flat and decorative style is epitomized by the *Siege of Lanka*, which was completed about 1730.

With an influx of Mughal artists, the depiction of colour in Pahari painting became more subtle. Flesh tone could now be rendered realistically, though there was as yet no attempt at perspective. Symbolism, especially erotic-symbolism, was still an important element.

The Pahari style of painting spread to some 35 hill states in Punjab. But the most important was Kangra, where the Raja Sansar Chand established an important school of painting in 1780. Sansar Chand was forced from power by the Sikhs in 1810, but withdrew to Sujanpur with his artists, who continued work under his patronage until 1823. Their paintings show that Sansar Chand was obsessed with two things — Krishna and female beauty. The Kangra school of painting became highly influential. When Sansar's son, Anirodh Chand, fled south to avoid being forced to marry a Sikh princess, he established a new school of art at **Garhwal**.

Once the Sikhs had consolidated their power in Punjab, they developed a taste for miniature paintings, especially those with military themes. But with the **British domination** of the subcontinent miniature painting fell from grace. Indian art became corrupted by a desire to please the new British patrons and much Indian scholarship was lost. Nevertheless, some of India's new rulers developed a sympathy for and an understanding of Indian art, and British connoisseurs and archaeologists slowly began to rediscover its remarkable history.

A miniature of the Garwhal school, 'Queen Prepared by her Servants'

HISTORICAL EVENTS	DATES	ART
Indus civilisation	About 2500-1500 BC	Painted pottery Inscribed seals Statuettes
Arrival of the Aryans Vedic India	About 1500-500 BC	
Evolution of Vedism towards Brahmanism Foundation of Buddhism and Jainism	6th century BC	
Expedititon of Alexander the Great Maurya dynasty Shunga dynasty	End of 4th century - 1st century BC	Asoka Pillars Earliest Buddhist art Stupas; excavated sanctuaries Buddha represented by symbols
Kushan dynasty Andhra dynasty	1st-4th centuries AD	Appearance of the image of the Buddha Graeco-Buddhist art The Mathura style The Amaravati style
Gupta dynasty	4th-6th centuries	Gupta style, the high point of Indian art Beginning of Brahmanic art First free-standing temples
Beginning of the Arab invasions	8th century	Post-Gupta style Pallava style Pala style
End of Buddhism in India Foundation of the Sultanate of Delhi	12th century	Late Buddhist works of the Pala style Dravidian style
Muslims in the Deccan Dravidian kingdom of Vijayanagar	14th-16th centuries	Indo-Persian art Dravidian style
Mughal Empire	16th-18th centuries	Indo-Persian art Mughal and Rajput schools of miniature painting Dravidian style

**'Krishna Playing a Flute', a
fine example of Pahari art
from Basohli, *circa* 1710**

Acknowledgements

Bridgeman Art Library / Fitzwilliam Museum. University of Cambridge 24 / National Museum of India frontispiece, frontispiece tracing, 12, 14, 15, 17, 18, 20, 34, 35, 41 right, 44, 45, 46, 47, 63, 91 / Victoria & Albert Museum 90, 94

J Allan Cash Photolibrary endpapers, 6, 48, 50/51, 76, 80, 80 tracing, 85

Werner Forman Archive 54/55, 74/75, 81 / British Museum 31/32 / M.H. de Young Memorial Museum, San Francisco 65 / Private Collection 4/5

Edgar Knobloch 8/9

Robert Harding Picture Library 11, 27, 32 tracing, 32/33, 36, 38, 39, 40, 42/43, 48 tracing, 49, 52/53, 52, 56/57, 58, 60/61, 62, 66/67, 68, 69, 71, 72, 73, 77, 78/79, 82, 97 / National Museum of Pakistan 10, 13, 16, 16 tracing, 19 / Sarnath Museum 22/23, 29

Reed International Books Ltd. / British Musem 89 / Musée Guimet 41 left / Victoria & Albert Museum front jacket, 64 tracing, 64, 83, 84, 86/87, 88, 93